Outer Limits

For a child's mind, in time and space

DAVE LEWIS

authorHOUSE®

AuthorHouse™
1663 Liberty Drive
Bloomington, IN 47403
www.authorhouse.com
Phone: 1 (800) 839-8640

Published by AuthorHouse 05/25/2017

ISBN: 978-1-5246-9434-0 (sc)
ISBN: 978-1-5246-9433-3 (e)

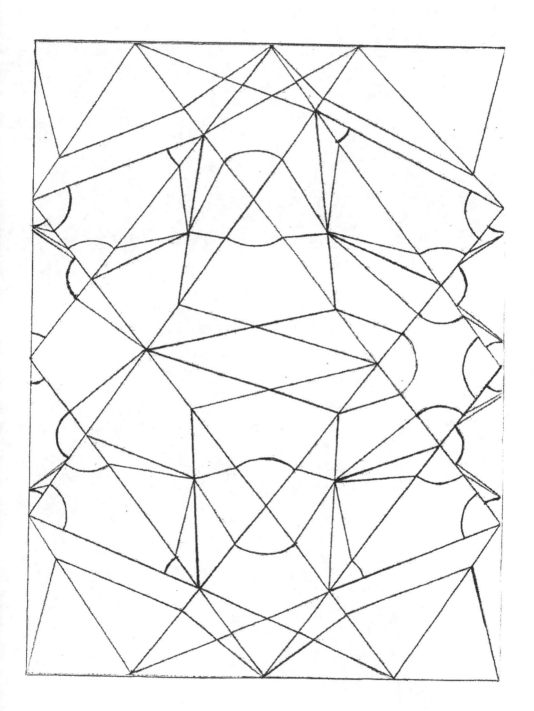

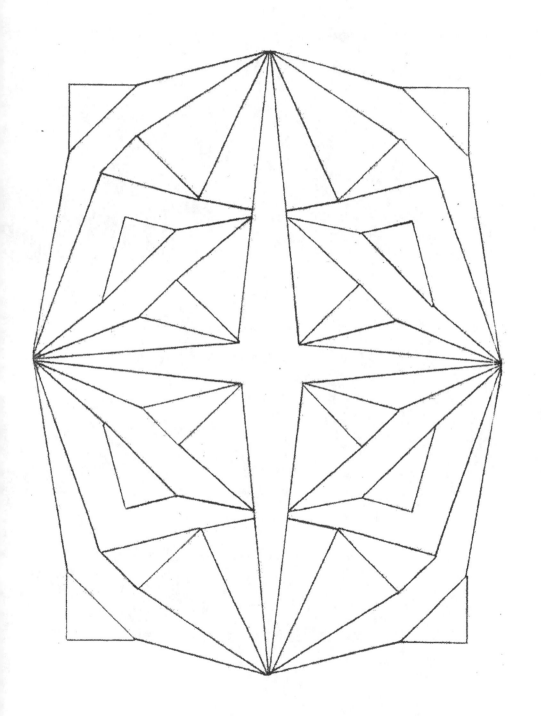

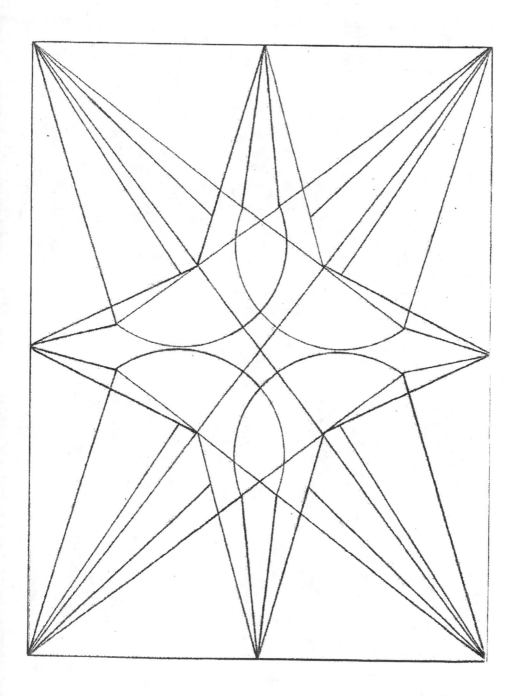

Printed in the United States
By Bookmasters